Rockin' The Rock
A Kid's Guide To the Rock Of Gibraltar

Photography By John D. Weigand
Poetry By Penelope Dyan

Bellissima Publishing, LLC
Jamul, California
www.bellissimapublishing.com

copyright © 2012 by Penny D. Weigand & John D. Weigand

All rights reserved. No part of this book may be
reproduced or transmitted in any form or by any means,
electronic or mechanical, including photocopying,
recording, or by any other means, or by any information or
storage retrieval system, without permission from the publisher.

ISBN 978-1-61477-037-4
First Edition

"What are men to rocks and mountains?"

Jane Austen, Pride and Prejudice

Rockin' The Rock
Bellissima Publishing, LLC

Introduction

Gibraltar is a British territory on the south end of the Iberian Peninsula's Mediterranean entrance. It's total area is 2.6 square miles, and it borders on the north with Andalusia, Spain. The Rock of Gibraltar is its major landmark. At its foot of the "Rock" is a densely populated city of almost 30,000 people. An Anglo-Dutch force captured Gibraltar from Spain in 1704 during the War of the Spanish Succession. The territory of the "Rock" was ceded to Great Britain "in perpetuity" under the 1713 Treaty of Utrecht. It became the base for the Royal Navy. Today, its economy is based on tourism, finance and shipping. Sovereignty of Gibraltar is at issue in Anglo-Spanish relations, because Spain assets a claim to the territory. However, the people of Gibraltar have rejected proposals for Spanish sovereignty, once in a 1967 referendum, and again in 2002. Under its 2006 constitution, Gibraltar governs all of its own affairs. However, the powers of defense and foreign relations remain the responsibility of the UK Government. To understand Gibraltar, one needs to talk to its people and see everything it has to offer. Look for Penelope Dyan music videos that go with this book, and for more from Bellissima Publishing, LLC, as you learn all you learn all you can about this place that gave rise to the expression: ". . . as strong as the rock of Gibraltar." The companion book to this book is "The Comeback Kids, Book 9, The Barbary Macaques of Gibraltar."

Rockin' The Rock
Bellissima Publishing, LLC

Rockin' The Rock
A Kid's Guide To The Rock Of Gibraltar

Photography By John D. Weigand
Poetry By Penelope Dyan

The rock rises from the sea
reminding us of who we can be.
We, too, can reach for the sky;
and we can rock the rock,
if we ONLY try!

You can drive to the rock,
or you can simply walk,
right over an airfield,
where you might have to stop
to let a plane take off
or to let a plane land.
This place (so far) is simply grand!

On the top of the rock you see
an ape walk across a stoney wall.
He's one of the apes of Gibraltar,
and he will NOT fall.
Below him you see La Linea, Spain
spread wide and far,
AND you can see it ALL from
your OWN cable car!

The main street is full of shops.
AND you can stop AND shop AND eat!
You are having so much fun!
The pavement flies beneath your feet!

There are dolphin of many a kind
swimming in surrounding waters deep.
The boat rocks gently back and forth,
and you NEARLY fall asleep!

You see a tiny chapel sweet.
It was built in 1560!
Oh my! How really neat!

There is a man on the street
blowing a great big bubble.
Your mom lets you watch,
but says, "Now, stay out of trouble."
You stop and take a long, long look.
You think, "I'll never see THIS
in ANY book!"

And then you remember that
lovely, lonely little monkey
upon the rock's hill,
sitting oh so VERY still.
You are happy the monkeys
are thriving up there.
And like Churchill, YOU want
to save monkeys EVERYWHERE!
But your mother says BEFORE you do,
you'll have to stop and tie your shoe,
or you MIGHT fall right on your face,
and your shoe will fly off into space!

You may never hear cannons roaring.
You may ONLY hear your dad snoring.
And even though you can ONLY hear
your baby sister's rattle,
you still imagine that great battle,
and the 1713 Treaty of Utrecht
that gave Britain this place,
and put a smile on that monkey's face!
The Barbary Macaques of Gibraltar
are protected and will forever stand,
upon the rock and upon the land.
And that makes you feel so very glad,
because without the monkeys
you would be sad, sad, sad, sad!

And as the lighthouse lights the way
for each boat,
that upon these waters come to float,
you think about everything
you have learned and heard,
and you wonder at the meaning of
each and EVERY word.

Upon this great rock the tailless monkey will continue to walk and sit. And he won't mind it one single bit.

The peacefulness of these waters
you leave far behind.
You think of a victory of
a quite different kind.
Man has helped nature now,
and you have learned exactly how.
Once of these monkeys,
there were only seven,
and now of these monkeys there are
three hundred MORE than eleven!
And it is All because of
Winston Churchill's decree,
to replenish them on this rock
by the sea.

In matters of style, swim with the current; in matters of principle, stand like a rock."

THOMAS JEFFERSON

www.ingramcontent.com/pod-product-compliance
Ingram Content Group UK Ltd.
Pitfield, Milton Keynes, MK11 3LW, UK
UKHW060134240426
12048UKWH00002B/36